PASSION
AND
PERFECTION

MEDITATIONS FOR HOLY WEEK & EASTER

W. NORMAN PITTENGER

ISBN 0-88028-044-1

Contents

Preface

The title of this little book of meditations has been chosen for a purpose and to make a particular point. Human anguish and death have been seen as exactly the opposite of divine perfection and human fulfilment. Our human experience, marked as it is by passion in both senses of that word — urgent and strong desire, on the one hand, and suffering and pain both mental and physical, on the other hand — has been contrasted with serene and changeless divine perfection. It is my conviction that Christian faith sees the situation in a very different fashion.

For that faith, I should urge, the divine reality we call God is *not* serene and changeless, immutable and impassible, unaffected by what goes on in the world. Some religious philosophies, some theologies, some ways of envisaging things, may and do talk in that way. But Christians ought never to do so. If the Christian faith is true, then we must declare without hesitation that in the total reality of Jesus Christ, witnessed to us in the New Testament and confirmed in continuing Christian living, we are given a disclosure in concrete historical action, of what God is *always* up to and hence what God *always* is. Or to put it in another way: Christian faith should be concerned to proclaim that we may, indeed that we must, generalize from that particular instance, that event in the world's history, so that what was acted out there becomes the key or clue to what is the deepest truth in the entire cosmos. God, who is the supremely worshipful, utterly dependable, inescapably unsurpassable reality, is to be known, and responded to, as passionate in both senses: God is utterly strong desire *and* God shares in suffering, pain, and anguish. The divine victory, which Easter celebrates, is not in spite of, nor the contradiction of, what took place on Good Friday; but it is the validation and confirmation of that day — certainly to all appearances a very *bad* day, yet a day which (as T.S. Eliot puts it in *Four Quartets*) "we call *good.*"

The material here published was originally delivered in a number of parishes. I wish to single out three; I name them because their rectors were especially kind to me during the time I was with them: St. George's Church in Schenectady, New York, and its then rector, Darwin Kirby; Christ Church in Rolla, Missouri, and its rector, Joseph Carlo; and St. Paul's Church in Cleveland Heights, Ohio, and its then rector Chave MacCracken. I am grateful to these priests and their people for the privilege of speaking to them. It is my hope that what was said on those occasions may be of help to others who wish to make sense, in their own lives, of the central point in historical Christian faith: the passion, death, and resurrection of Jesus Christ.

Norman Pittenger

King's College,
Cambridge, England

1.

The Sunday of the Passion: Palm Sunday

An ancient Christian hymn, which comes to us from the early days of the Christian Church, is often sung on Palm Sunday. In it are the lines:

The royal banners forward go and
God is reigning from the Tree.

Another hymn, usually sung as a Palm Sunday processional, begins with the words, "All glory, laud, and honour, to thee, Redeemer King." In all these, Jesus Christ is addressed as King, but as a king who reigns from the Cross and not from a heavenly throne with 'all passion spent.' On Palm Sunday we celebrate the beginning of the final week in our Lord's life in Palestine; it was a week which ended in death. Here is tragedy, we say; yet it is tragedy with a difference.

The tragedy is acted out in concrete events. It is horrible, appalling. Yet somehow it is also triumphant, for 'the royal banners' *do* proclaim that its central figure is not to be pitied but rather to be acclaimed, that he is worthy of worship and adoration. Like all tragedy the spectacle moves us profoundly. At the same time, again as in all tragedy, there is given to us a purification — what Aristotle calls *catharsis* — as we seek to share in what is going on.

The great Greek tragedies, on the one hand, and the tragedies of William Shakespeare (like *Lear, Hamlet, Othello, Macbeth*), on the other, help us to penetrate into the depths of human experience, as their protagonists undergo rejection, contradiction, denial, and death. Those tragedies are literary creations. The events of Holy Week are not literary creations but the enactment on the stage of human history of that which the dramatists — as well as many poets, novelists, and artists — have discerned and represented. And what is it which these have grasped and which in Holy Week is enacted? The answer to that question is this. Genuine triumph and victory are to be found, not in the denial of the anguish known in human experience, but on the contrary in the acceptance of that anguish, so that it is seen as a disclosure of the deepest drive and thrust in the universe, of the divine way of doing and being, of God's very self. God is not only *like* that; that *is* God's true nature and character. It is *God* who is 'reigning from the Tree', says Christian faith, not merely the best of men forced to undergo exquisite pain.

Thus when we are asked to say something about the distinctive quality of Christian faith, we have an answer. The answer is not that Christian people are better than others; obviously they are not. Nor is it that they are more profoundly religious than others; again obviously they are not. Nor is it that Christian theory or speculation is more adequate to what we humans experience and know; this is not necessarily the case. Nor is it that only those who 'profess and call themselves Christians' are to be or can be or have been 'saved,' as the phrase goes. To talk like that is to be pretentious and self-congratulatory and in any event it is presuming altogether too much.

What is distinctive about the Christian tradition and our life within it is that it affirms something about *God* — a something that may have been hinted at, guessed about, discerned in theory, elsewhere; but a something which in Christian faith is declared with power as sure truth. What is this? It is that God is always caring, redeeming, reconciling; *and* that this is disclosed in act, in historical reality, in Jesus on his Cross. There, says Christian faith, God is disclosed to us human children as sheer Love; God is 'the fellow-sufferer who understands' because God has been participant in our darkest hours. "He leads us through no darker rooms than he's been through before," says Richard Baxter's poem.

But it is not only that this is declared to us and disclosed for us. It is that God is there *at work,* not remote and coming as a one-time visitor to the world. And what God is doing there tells us what God is always doing. Furthermore, in that doing God is releasing divine love to us, making available for use the divine power of loving, so that we may become in a small and human fashion God's 'co-creators,' God's 'fellow-workers,' in the great love-story which is the creation. "Love divine, all loves excelling," as Charles Wesley's great hymn puts it, is let loose into the world in Jesus' life and death and in the 'rising again' which we shall celebrate on Easter Day, to be with us now and to be ours forever.

As we go on through Holy Week, our minds should dwell on this reality. We only glimpse it very partially, to be sure. But if and as we dwell upon it, and center our thinking and willing and feeling upon it, it will become more and more "the master-light of all our seeing" and enable us to know more and more what is the way, which is both truth and life.

2.

Holy Thursday

Suppose that the 'man from Mars' should turn up on this earth. He would look around and observe what we humans are doing and saying. He would see all sorts of things which to him might seem very odd. And he might ask one of us to tell him what it is that many of us are doing when we go to a gathering of men and women and children on one day of the week and engage in what we call an act of worship. He might say, "What is this Christian business which seems to so many of you important and rewarding?"

How would you answer his question? You might recite to him one of the creeds which have come down to us from our past. You might talk about a pattern of behaviour which can be called 'Christian.' You might hand him a copy of the Bible, with the New Testament indicated as of crucial significance. But I think that the best way to answer his question would be to bring him along with you to a Christian gathering in which the sacrament of the Lord's Supper, the Holy Eucharist, the Communion Service, the Mass — call it what you will — was being celebrated. Having got him there, you might say to him, '*That* is what the Christian business is all about; *that* is Christianity visibly expressed and acted out.'

If you did this, you would be doing the right thing. For the simple fact is that in this sacramental rite "the whole of our redemption is gathered up." Those are words from the great medieval Christian thinker Thomas Aquinas; I am sure that what St. Thomas said is the truth about the eucharistic action.

So let us now try to spell out more precisely what the Lord's Supper means — and it is appropriate that we should do this on Holy Thursday, because this is the day when the Christian community remembers, with a special directness, what happened on "the night before [Jesus] was betrayed." In a very remarkable way, what happened on that night, in the Upper Room where Jesus was with his disciples, is the beginning, on a particular occasion, of what has been happening ever since among Christian people. When I was young, I was told that 'it's the Mass that *matters.*' That was a rather 'high Church' saying, I suppose; none the less, I am sure that it was a true saying. How does this sacrament matter?

In the first place, it matters because the Eucharist is 'the continual remembrance' of the total event of Jesus Christ. Sometimes this remembrance has been talked about as if it were confined to 'the sacrifice of the *death* of Christ.' But to confine it to the death is to forget the insight of a medieval saint that "the whole life of Christ is the mystery of the Cross." Christ's entire existence, from his birth through his days of teaching and doing in Palestine, through his betrayal and trial, through his dying on Calvary, to the victory which Christian faith has discerned and which on Easter Day we commemorate — Christ's whole existence is 'remembered' in the celebration of the Lord's Supper. We may be glad that in most of the contemporary revisions of the liturgy the point is made clear; those revisions do not neglect the total fact by concentrating only on the crucifixion.

Now the word 'remembrance' can be misunderstood, as if it meant only some pious reverie, as if we turned back in our thinking and attended to something that happened in the past and is now over and done with. For the Jewish people, however, 'remembrance' had a much more profound significance than that; it still does today. When Jews gather for the *seder,* the meal which they observe to commemorate the Passover, that is their deliverance from Egypt and their crossing into the Sinaitic peninsula before they entered the land of Canaan, they are not primarily intent upon an event in the distant past. On the contrary, they believe that in the *seder* meal, as they re-enact what they believe took place long ago, the reality of what then took place is made present to them in their contemporary existence. What might have been the dead past becomes for them the living present. So it is in Christian remembrance of Christ in the Eucharist.

When the old song asks, "Were you there when they crucified my Lord," the answer a Christian must make is, "Yes, I was there and I am there, when the bread is broken and the wine shared in the Lord's Supper." The past events from which Christian faith took its rise are no longer merely in the past. They are present, known, experienced, and lived, as the Eucharist is celebrated. Hence 'memorial' or 'remembrance' becomes 'present-ness' or a 'here-with-us-now' experience.

The Lord is no longer remembered simply in the sense of his being thought about. He is remembered because he is now present, to be for his people their nourishing and their strengthening. *How* this happens is a matter for speculation; *that* it happens is the deliverance of Christian experience. That is the second point about the Eucharist. There is a third point — and that is the offering of ourselves, "our souls and bodies," back to God in association with the Lord's own self-giving. Of course we cannot offer Christ again, as if we had some control over him; but we can be made participant in that sacrifice, by his will and in response to his action, as we become "very members, incorporate in the mystical Body" of Christ, united with him and given to share in what he himself is doing.

So, in the fourth place, we are in communion with God as defined in Christ — defined in Christ because God is enacted in the event we are celebrating with its focus upon what God has "determined, dared, and done" there "for us men and for our salvation." If we are thus in communion with God as defined in Christ, we are also in communion with our fellow-humans as they too are defined in Christ. Which is to say, we are caught up into a fellowship which is not based upon the 'varied and manifold changes of this mortal life' but is grounded in our human 'en-christedness,' because (as St. Paul puts it dozens of times) we are ourselves 'in Christ' — and so also are our brothers and sisters. For the moment we are living in love because we are permitted to live in Love — in the former instance we are with our brethren in charity and in labour for justice in the world; in the latter instance we are in God who is Love, declared, defined, and disclosed in the Lord with whom we are now united "by faith with thanksgiving."

Last of all, we are given a job to do — in traditional words, we are 'sent' to be God's instruments in the divine work of 'amorization,' or love-making, reflecting in our small way the divine Love in its never-failing amorization of the world. We shall fail in this, because we are fallible and defective men and women. Yet we can accept the amazing fact that we have been accepted, just as we are, by God as shown and known in what Jesus was and did; and having now accepted our own acceptance, we can learn slowly and even painfully to accept others, to accept the world, and to accept God's ceaseless and often hidden movement towards men, women, and children, seeking them out, bringing them back to God and establishing among them sovereign rule of justice and love.

That is what the 'man from Mars' might be enabled to discern as he sees Christian people gathered together again and again to celebrate the Eucharist: God's self-giving, God's self-enactment in the Man Jesus, God's making available the love which went to the Cross but was not defeated by the Cross, God's making a new community whose characteristic mark is love-in-act, God's working through that community and its members to bring the whole creation towards the sovereign reign in which the Love that was crucified has become the Love that is triumphant, in men and women and for men and women and by a Man who is one of us.

3.

Good Friday

What a strange thing it is to call this Friday 'good.' For many centuries ago, on a Friday, men in high positions of authority put to death, in an especially cruel way, a young man whom succeeding ages have seen to be the best man, the most admirable man, this world has ever known. How odd, then, to commemorate the day of his death by calling it 'good.'

There is something else, too. Those of us who are Christians, or dare to think ourselves to be such, or would like to believe that we are such, have the conviction, however faintly we assert it, that we see in that "strange man upon his Cross" (to use some words of Father George Tyrrell) not only the best and most admirable and most loving man this world has ever known. We see in him the action of God in this world, in a signal and decisive fashion. We call him 'our Lord' and by this we affirm that in him the supreme reality, the basic thrust and drive working through all things in the creation, that One we call God, is present and is acting, in a way that we proclaim to be unparalleled elsewhere, a way that is so special that it calls forth in us much more than admiration of human goodness. It evokes from us sheer worship.

Charles Lamb was once part of a company who were discussing the person in history whom they would most wish to meet.

Many names were mentioned but Lamb was silent. Then, as the gathering came to an end, he said this: "I can think of but one name. If Shakespeare were to come into this room, we should all rise and wish to take his hand. If that One were to come in, we should fall on our knees and try to kiss the hem of his garment." That is the response which this Jesus has evoked from countless millions of men and women. For them, and for us, God is there in him; somehow or other the divine reality is enacted in that human reality.

Thus on that terrible Friday centuries ago, human beings like you and me put to death One who was not merely the best of our race; more horribly, they put to death, in an agonizing way of dying, the One in whom God was present and in whom God was acting. This is nothing short of appalling; and so we may well ask, once again, How *can* we call this Friday 'good'?

Yet as T.S. Eliot put it in a poem which has already been quoted in an earlier meditation, we *do* call it good, despite its horror and despite its anguish. Doubtless the people who crucified Jesus had the best intention and the sincere conviction that it was the right thing to do. They were like us in this respect, for very often we do evil things in the belief that we are doing the right things to preserve the *status quo,* to defend established ideas, or to assert our belief in something which we take to be important. But those people did commit this horrible deed. So again we must ask how it is that succeeding centuries have dared to call this day a 'good' day.

First, we put it that way because as Christian people we believe that in the crucifixion of Jesus God was sharing human suffering, human anguish, human experience of rejection and condemnation. The unique thing about Christian faith is just this. For those who share that faith God is not remote and unconcerned in the affairs of the world. For Christian faith God is not one who dwells entirely apart from our human life, with its sorrow as well as its joy, its agony as well as its ecstacy. On the contrary, Christian faith declares that God is self-

18

identified with our human life and knows, from inside it, that sorrow and joy, that agony and ecstacy.

This is why we can say, in the words of the Psalmist, "If I go down into hell" — into the place and time of anguish — "*thou* art there also." We are not alone in such moments. God is there, as 'the fellow-sufferer who understands' because God shares our experience. We need then never be afraid, because we are convinced that God is with us, even in our worst moments of despair, frustration, and pain. Because this day manifests God's being with us, we can call this Friday 'good.'

In the second place, the God who is with us is disclosed in Jesus, as he hangs upon his cross, as "pure unbounded Love." For it is the divine Love, and that alone, which could and would thus identify itself with us in such an intimate and all-encompassing fashion. A genuine lover is always one with those whom he or she loves, whether in their joy or in their sorrow, their agony or their ecstacy. "God is Love," says St. John in his first letter. He could say this, as we can say it after him, not as an interesting speculation or as a splendid theory, but as an unmistakable fact — because in that Man on his cross, brought to that cross by other human beings, God has demonstrated vividly and plainly that he loves us enough to become one with us in all that we experience in our life on this earth. And thus this day is 'good.'

Lastly, the Love which was there present and acting — or better, the great cosmic Lover who was there present and acting — was not overcome or defeated or vanquished or destroyed by what happened on that Friday centuries ago. The cross of Jesus has about it, not the negative quality of defeat, but the positive quality of victory. You and I are not to 'pity Jesus,' as we might pity someone who has been a martyr to a good cause. You and I *acclaim* Jesus as the One in whom 'the victory o'er death is won.' For Good Friday and Easter Day belong together for us who are Christians or who wish to think of ourselves as attempting to be Christians. It is not as if Easter

19

Day, with its proclamation of Jesus risen from death, were to be seen as the contradiction or reversal of Good Friday. That might be true of some serial story in a periodical where the next-to-the-last episode is marked by anguish but the last episode has simply changed that anguish into a time 'when they lived happily ever after.' No, Easter Day is the confirmation and validation, not the contradiction or reversal, of that Friday.

Why is this so? Simply because, as we shall be seeing, on Easter Day God acted as if to write over the cross the words, 'That is what I always am.' Love like that, God's love, "Love divine, all loves excelling," *is* victorious in any and through any and every mortal, finite, human circumstance.

Can you and I believe that? If we cannot or do not, we have not discerned the most profound affirmation of the faith which we claim to profess. If we can believe it, we have the assurance, unshakeable and firm, that "neither life nor death, neither height nor depth," indeed nothing at all, "can separate us from the love of God which was in Christ Jesus our Lord."

4.

Father, Forgive Them

"The entire life of Christ was the mystery of the cross," said a medieval saint. *(Tota vita Christi mysterium crucis)* We must keep in mind the truth expressed in those words, because there is the danger that we shall think that the crucifixion was, so to say, something added on to Jesus' life in the world, a kind of extra which had no relation to what had gone on before. On the contrary, the whole of Jesus' life — his doings and sayings as these are told us in the four gospels — was a continuing dedication and self-giving to God and to his fellow-humans. That means that it was all a sacrifice, an offering, a sharing of himself with others. That was the kind of life, a life of sacrificial offering for others, which came to its climactic point on Calvary. On the cross Jesus died, doing there in a supreme and concentrated fashion what he had been doing through all his days. When we consider the words which the earliest Christians believed he had spoken from the cross, we must see that they are not only 'words from the cross' but also words which tell us plainly what Jesus always was, what he was always doing; in fact, they disclose to us the inner spirit or quality of Jesus himself. That is why their importance cannot be exaggerated.

'Father, forgive them, for they know not what they do' (Luke 23:24).

Jesus is here shown as praying for the people who had condemned him to death and who now were crucifying him: the religious leaders of the nation, the Roman civil authority, the soldiers who crowned him with thorns, the crowds who spat upon him and jeered at him. Those people were not different from you and me. We can identify with them, as a contemporary way of talking phrases it. In us too there is narrow prejudice, sense of pride, conviction of the rightness of our own ideas, readiness to follow the crowd, however terrible may be the mass-feeling which leads men and women to behave in reprehensible ways.

Let us not think for a moment that we would have acted differently had we been in the shoes of those people in Jerusalem two thousand years ago. If we do think that we are so much better than they, this thought of ours only demonstrates how little we really know about ourselves at the deepest level and how presumptuous and proud we can often be about ourselves, our motives, and our actions. In the traditional way of saying it, we are all of us sinners; it would be absurd and blind to claim that we are not.

But Jesus prays that those people shall be forgiven; and in that prayer of his you and I are also included. We too need to be forgiven, both for what we do and for what we fail to do: "we have done those things which we ought not to have done and we have not done those things which we ought to have done." *And* "there is no health *in us*." We are sick people and we should honestly admit it. Our sickness is our self-content, our pride, our lovelessness. We need to be made healthy, made whole, for that is what forgiveness is all about. In *us,* in our little human lives, there is no health; even the best of us, as we think of ourselves in our blindness, are in need of the new life which is health.

Have you ever thought that never do we humans sin so boldly as when we do it with 'a good conscience?' The Frenchman Pascal once said that. If ever the saying were true, surely it was true of the people who brought Jesus to his death. They were misguided, ill-informed, zealous for the religious tradition which they had inherited and which they valued so highly. They were concerned for law and order and the maintenance of things as they had been. In a way they were very good people. But they did not know what they were doing. So it is with us, much of the time. Jesus *did* know and *does* know; and because he had this knowledge, he could understand why they did what they did. Like you and me, they did the wrong things for the best of motives — or at least for motives that seemed to them entirely good.

We do not know ourselves, in the deepest sense of knowing. Frequently we ask, after some act that in retrospect is seen as appallingly wrong, "How could I have done that? That wasn't something I should have done at all, had I realized what it was going to bring about." For we are dreadfully ignorant, both about ourselves and about what we are likley to do. It is only God "unto whom all hearts are open, all desires known, and from whom no secrets are hid." With us, we never know in any really complete way what our desires really are; even our own hearts are not entirely open to us and our secrets are often deeply hidden. This is why we can hardly ever succeed in truly knowing ourselves, much less truly knowing other people. It is also why we dare not presume to sit in judgement on others and why we can scarcely pretend properly to judge ourselves. Only God can know us and judge us, as well as other people, as we all really are.

What is more, only God can really forgive. Jesus prayed to his heavenly Father for those people who were crucifying him; he prayed that God, who alone knows and can rightly judge because God truly knows, will forgive them. How about us? Can we forgive, or rather can we ask God to forgive, the people who have wronged us, misused us, hurt us, made us miserable, given us pain, damaged our inner being? How about our family, wife and husband and children and parents and

23

lovers? How about our friends and neighbours? How about our supposed friends and those who are our enemies? Can you and I bring ourselves to be forgiving towards those who have done wrong to us or who we think have done wrong to us? Can we sincerely ask God to forgive them?

The answer to such questions, so far as you and I are concerned in our human ignorance and our human selfishness, has to be "No." *We* cannot forgive, in and of ourselves; we cannot bring ourselves to ask God to forgive, if we are asking this in our own strength alone. But God can and God does forgive; and if you and I are caught up into the divine *chesed,* as the Jews phrased it, into God's 'loving-mercy,' God can forgive through us. Of course God can. Otherwise, how could we ourselves have been forgiven and how could we dare to say this about ourselves? Our faith tells us that we have indeed been forgiven, however sinful, wrong, perverse, nasty, disagreeable we may be. Let us therefore, open our selves, our little imperfect hearts and lives, so that the forgiveness which we have received from God may flow through us in forgiveness to others.

"Father, forgive them." God does just that. And God would have us become instruments to bring that forgiveness to others.

5.

Today Thou Shalt Be With Me In Paradise

We all know the story of the 'penitent thief,' or as we ought to call him the 'penitent bandit-leader,' who presumably had been taken in custody about the same time as Jesus' arrest and had been condemned to death, along with a companion, at the same place as Jesus. The story tells how he refused to join with his fellow-criminal in cursing the third figure, Jesus. Somehow, it would seem from the way the gospels speak, he had recognized in Jesus an innocent person who has committed no offense worthy of death. Perhaps he had heard stories about Jesus as having been accused of pretense as a king. In any event, he is represented as saying to Jesus, "Master, remember me when you come into your kingdom." To which Jesus made the reply which is the second saying remembered by tradition as having been uttered from the cross: "Today you shall be with me in Paradise." (Luke 23:43)

It is difficult to know the precise meaning of this saying, so far as Jesus himself in his human mind (for he was certainly truly a man and hence *had* a human mind) would have intended it. New Testament scholars have differed about this, as they do about so many points in the gospels. Some think it simply to be an affirmation that soon, indeed on that very day, Jesus and the rebel leader will both have died. Others think that Jesus was giving the man an assurance that they would be together in an existence beyond death. For you and me, I suggest, the words say something that is more important, even if we cannot grasp their concrete historical significance. What is that? May it not be a way of asserting that our human destiny is bound up in some fashion with this Jesus and with what he was doing on the cross? Let me put this by noting that Christian faith is sure that when we die, as all of us must, we do not pass into utter nothingness, as if we had never existed at all. Rather, we go 'home to God,' as it were, where Jesus has gone before us; and hence we are 'with Jesus' in the very life of God.

To be a Christian is to be confident that we have been so truly incorporated into, made one with, Jesus, that where he is, there we shall also be. And if Jesus, bearing as he does upon his person "those dear tokens of his passion," those wounds which are the sign of his full sharing in human suffering and death: if *that* Jesus is with the Father, forevermore part of God's own life, then we also can trust that we shall be with the Father and in Jesus made a very part of God's life.

Just how this may be we do not know. To my mind many people have assumed far too easily that they can make a precise and accurate map of human destiny. They have talked as if they were privy to the mind of God and hence know exactly what happens to men and women at and after death. Such an attitude seems to me to be presumptuous and even blasphemous; we do not have, nor with our finite minds can we hope to acquire, the sort of knowledge about these matters which some would like to have. I think that it is better so. There is great mystery here and we ought to respect that mystery.

Yet we can be confident of at least one thing, which is the really important thing. We can be sure that as now we are known and loved by God, so also we shall be known and loved by him forever. We can trust the great Lover of men and women and children to do what is best for us human children. God does not let us down; God is always trustworthy and God's care for us is never-failing. Thus, to be 'in Paradise' can mean for us that one thing: "when we wake up after his likeness, we shall be satisfied," in whatever way God wills this. God *will* do for us all that God *can* do for us.

One way of expressing this Christian conviction is through a deep understanding of God's *memory* of us human children. In the thought of Jewish people memory, as we have said, is no pious reverie; it is a way of making-alive in the present moment what has taken place in the past. For God to remember, then, is for God to make us alive in a fashion that is appropriate to the divine nature. Our memory is fallible and weak; God's must be perfect and strong. For us Christians the celebration of the Eucharist is the way in which the past becomes present. Here is memory or remembrance par excellence. *God's* memory is like that, only in God it is raised to the highest possible fullness and reality.

The bandit-leader's plea, "Lord, remember me," was met by Jesus' declaration that he *will* be remembered. We can say that he will be remembered in God, for what he was and for what he did; and thus to be remembered is not to go into nothingness but rather to go into the life of God. This is everlasting life, because God is the Everlasting One. Hence we need not fear for ourselves, nor for those whom we love. We can rest in that confidence; and instead of being over-anxious about such matters, we can be sure that God will do for us, as God does always for everyone, "more than we can ask or think." God has bound us, in Jesus, in an unbreakable communion. You and I and all the faithful departed are joined in the communion of saints, with Jesus and his blessed Mother and all others who have been drawn into God's life through Jesus Christ our Lord. Surely that is enough for anybody.

6.

Woman Behold Thy Son...
Son, Behold Thy Mother

In this word from the cross we have what many of us think to be one of the most tender and moving bits of the gospel record. It is told only in the Fourth Gospel, that of St. John. (John 19:26 ff) Here we see Jesus showing his love for his mother who had conceived and born him, and for his friend who (that same evangelist tells us) was "the disciple whom Jesus loved." All this means that Jesus shared fully in our human affections, both familial and friendly; and by that sharing we are given the confidence we need to enter more deeply and more completely into just such human loving.

The poet John Keats spoke once of the importance for us of what he called 'trust' in the 'the heart's affections.' The English theologian Austin Farrer had the courage to say that it is precisely by such a trust that we come — and only by that trust can come — to some grasp of what is the significance of our saying that God is Love. Not, mind you, that God is merely 'loving' true as that is; but that God's very essence, God's 'root-attribute,' is not self-centred existence, not sufficiency to exist even if nothing else or nobody else existed, but sheer Love itself. "God's essence and his very self," as Cardinal Newman's hymn *Praise to the Holiest in the heights* so splendidly puts it, is nothing other than Love, utter self-giving Love. To believe that

29

fact, in a world with so much evil and wrong in it, is surely the most courageous thing any of us can achieve. But thanks be to God, you and I, as those who profess and call ourselves Christian, can and do believe it. We believe it not because it is a nice thought or a beautiful theory, but because God has so loved us that he (or she, for we can use that pronoun too) gave us Jesus. And why did God do that? In order that the divine Love declared and enacted in our humanity, in that same Jesus, might make it possible for us truly *to live,* not just to 'exist' as somewhat sophisticated mortal creatures.

Having said that, I now wish to turn to another matter. I want to suggest to you that for many of us our religious faith has been sadly impoverished because we have not been allowed to see that in his blessed mother, to whom Jesus commended his friend as he also commended his mother to that friend, we have a guarantee of God's concern for women as well as for men. What is even more important, in that same Mary we have the symbol that represents for us the fullness of human response to God, never excelled save in the human existence of Jesus himself.

Far too much of the religion of many of us is overly-masculine, overly patriarchal, talking too much of deity in terms of a male conception of governor or ruler, and far too little in terms of tender affection and maternal love. Julian of Norwich, English mystic of the Middle Ages, called God *both* Mother and Father and on some occasions (in that superb piece of writing, *The Shewings* [or revelations] *of Dame Julian*) dared even to address Jesus as her mother as well as her brother.

So I urge that a devotion to St. Mary — to 'our Lady' as she is styled in the more Catholic tradition of Christianity — can be an enormous enrichment of our religious faith. I urge that we should give her a place in our thinking and praying. We may profit greatly if we make our own the ancient salutation, from St. Luke's gospel, "Hail, Mary, full of grace, blessed art thou among women and blessed is the fruit of thy womb,

Jesus." And why should we not go on to ask that she, who is the mother of our Lord, may "pray for us, now and in the hour of our death."

We know very little, almost nothing, of the life of St. Mary. Many of the stories told about her, apart from the slight references in the gospel narratives, are more legendary than factual. I concede that this is so. Yet some of those stories are what Italians would style *ben trovato*: 'worth telling." They are suggestive in their pointing to the devotion of this mother to her son, as well as of his devotion to her who was his mother. The English divines of the seventeenth century used to say that it is right for Christians to give to St. Mary 'all devotion short of the worship which is due to God alone.' That seems to me exactly right; and that is why I venture to commend to you a chastened but genuine devotion to the one who in being the mother of our Lord is also (precisely because we are knit together with him in one body of faith, worship, and life) *our* mother too — the one who in St. Thomas Aquinas' great phrase was "the consenting cause of the incarnation," since it was by her response, in faith and obedience to the message of an angel, that Christ was conceived and born into this world of ours.

'The heart's affections,' of which John Keats spoke, must never be dismissed as only so much sentimentality. Doubtless much of our human affection is set upon things or persons that are not very worthy. We need to have those affections 'ordered,' to use St. Augustine's prayer: "Lord, order my loving" — that is, give it the right pattern and the right proportion. It is also true that when our affection is turned to those whom we can truly and rightly love, we are given 'a little bit of heaven' to enjoy even here and now in this mortal life. Few things are more deeply moving than the sight of two people who genuinely and unselfishly love one another. You can see it in their eyes, their gestures, their conduct. All the world loves a lover; you and I ought to find our hearts warmed when we see love in our midst. My old friend the novelist E.M. Forster used to say that the

31

trouble with us is not so much that our hearts are cold but that they are 'undeveloped.' That is tragic.

We can begin to 'develop' them by remembering the blessed Mother of Jesus; and from that remembrance we can ourselves learn to have the courage to trust our deepest affections and discover, to our delight and encouragement, that our own little lives have been hallowed and blessed.

7.

My God, My God, Why Hast Thou Forsaken Me?

This has often been called the hardest word uttered from the cross. For a great many the saying is both terrible and puzzling. Here we have what has been called 'a cry of dereliction,' a cry of sheer despair. Jesus was forsaken by his fellow-humans, yes; and that would be bad enough. But to be forsaken by *God* — to feel that his entire life had been given for a cause that now seemed to be only a failure — that was far worse.

We do not have any knowledge of what might be styled 'the psychology of Jesus,' with his innermost feelings. Certainly the words here seem to be an expression of inner loss as well as outer rejection by everyone, God included. Yet I should urge that, of all the words which early Christian tradition reported as spoken by Jesus as he died on Calvary, this is *for us* the most encouraging, heartening, and strengthening; it is for us the most reassuring and gives us profound confidence for our living in love: it offers us the most important of all possible insights into the heart of God. Or, to use a phrase from the Eucharist, it is supremely a 'comfortable word' — remembering always that when the first Anglican Prayer Book was compiled by Thomas Cranmer in the sixteenth century, the word 'comfortable' meant 'refreshing and invigorating,' and not, as it does for us today, 'ease' or anything of that pleasant kind.

Let us now think about this *comfortable* saying of Jesus: this word that is able to give to Christian believers refreshing, strengthening, and new vigour and courage: "My God, my God, why hast thou forsaken me?" (Matthew 27:26, Mark 15:34)

At first glance the word appears to be anything but what I have just said. It seems to represent the complete end of all that Jesus hoped for and purposed. It looks as if it were exactly that: *the end.* God was absent, or so it seemed; and Jesus must die entirely alone, forgotten as well as rejected. He would have been a failure, nothing more, nothing less.

However, we have to ask ourselves the question, "*Was* God absent?" Had God indeed forsaken Jesus? Our answer to the question depends upon how we think about Jesus himself. If we see him as only a man, doubtless the best and most loving man who ever lived but still only human, then it is the case that he was "despised and rejected" both by his fellow-humans and by God. But if in and through that genuinely human life, which was "bone of our bone and flesh of our flesh," there was a working and a presence of God in human life; if in Jesus, as Christians have always dared to affirm, there was an activity of God as well as of man, something of divinity as well as full humanity — if *that* is true, then God was not absent from Jesus nor had God forsaken Jesus. On the contrary, God was more active and hence more present then and there than at any other moment in history.

So to the question, Where was God when Jesus hung dying in anguish on the cross? our Christian answer must be just this: God was there, there in Jesus; and God was there sharing fully and completely in the anguish which the Son endured. For it all depends on how we have come to think about God and about God's character or nature, about what model or picture we have of God. And how do we think about that God's way of acting in the world which is his creation?

Far too many of us who call ourselves Christian are much less than Christian in our thinking about these matters. We look

34

at God as an imperial Caesar or a cosmic dictator; or we look at God as the observer of the world but not personally involved in it; or we look at God as a moral ruler who demands of us creatures total obedience to an arbitrarily imposed divine law or commandment. Then indeed God may seem to be a 'moral monster,' as somebody has put it. But that is not the way in which we ought to picture God. It has nothing to do with the picture of God given us in what Whitehead called "the brief Galilean vision."

That vision does not show us a God who is benevolent now and again, perhaps but who is essentially remote from us and not involved with us. The truly Christian picture is very different. It shows us a God who is Love, Love that identifies itself passionately with the world and with us, Love that suffers as and when we suffer, Love that works indefatigably in human existence. Above all, it is a vision of Love that knows from its own experience, from the inside, what it is like to suffer the anguish of rejection, the despair that comes when everything and everybody has failed us, the dereliction through loss of hope that is the worst experience that any man or woman could be obliged to undergo.

Earlier in these meditations I quoted the Psalmist: "If I go down to hell, thou art there also." Now perhaps you will see the point. You and I can have no experience, good or bad, joyful or painful, in which God who is Love does not fully share. Because God shares it all, because God is in it all, we need never feel utterly lost, hopeless, or in complete despair. The reason is that Love like that — the Love 'that came down at Christmas' and worked through and in and with all that Jesus said and did and was — is in fact victorious. But it is victorious not in spite of, nor as the contradiction of, the terror we know and the anguish we feel. Rather, it is (as I have just said) indefatigable, which means that it never gives up; it is also indefeasible, which means that it can never be defeated. It is always with us, in the assurance of triumph.

Can you and I believe that, with heart and soul and mind? It is not easy to believe, which is why being a Christian demands a readiness to live in spite of consequence and in the face of evil. If we can believe it, we are indeed deeply Christian in our understanding. If we cannot or do not believe it, then we are in need of conversion. For to be a Christian is, in the last resort, nothing other than to share the abiding faith that life's mystery, which we cannot escape whoever or wherever we are, finds its meaning, as it finds also its true way to survive blessedly now and always, in a suffering *and* a triumph in the God who 'for us and for our salvation' is identified with the human lot, asking no special privileges and possessing no special information. "Thanks be to God, who giveth us the victory through our Lord Jesus Christ."

8.

I Thirst

How human it is to be thirsty! Few of our bodily experiences so vividly demonstrate the fact of our humanity. In every land, under every climate, under all conditions, men and women have need of something to drink, something that will slake the thirst of which, under these varying circumstances, they are so conscious — often painfully conscious.

Jesus was no exception to this. Like the rest of us, he could be genuinely thirsty in a physical sense. But very likely he was thirsty in still another and much deeper way. He was thirsty for the companionship of fellow-humans, with the need common to us all for relationships with others who will understand us, share with us their experiences as we share our own, and participate with us in our very existence as we wish to share in theirs.

In Latin the word *corpus* means 'body.' That is why we speak of 'corporal life,' bodily life, as an essential aspect of our humanity. But we also speak of 'corporate life,' by which we mean that we belong together as humans in what an Old Testament text calls "a bundle of life" — in this case, *social* life; quite as much as we are 'embodied' creatures who function through a physical as well as a more mental or spiritual way. Both our physical body and our social belonging are necessary to our full humanity. We need always to remember that if Jesus was indeed one of us, a genuine man, he must have known both the need for physical food and drink to nourish and support his body *and* the need for other people so that he might live in a truly human fashion. The former of these two needs is obvious enough. The latter may not be so obvious, yet it is just as real. The English poet and priest John Donne said many years ago that "no man is an island entire unto itself." Each one is part of "the main," a member of the human race who by necessity shares in the common life of humankind.

Thus we may properly take this word of Jesus from the cross as proof of the fullness of his belonging to the human race, like the rest of us. Whatever else we may feel obliged to say about him, this remains basic. Of course, as I have urged earlier, any Christian interpretation of Jesus which can claim to be true to the historical tradition of which we are part includes the joyous affirmation that in him there was a signal and decisive activity and presence of God — that is what the Christian ages have been trying to say when they have spoken of Jesus' 'divinity.' On the other hand, had he not also been utterly human — our brother as well as our Lord — he could not have done for us what we are sure that he has done: brought us close to God, 'redeemed us' as we say, without for a moment making us other than men and women who can now realize what it means, deeply and truly, to *be* just that. God does not want us to be *angels*, defined as they have been by St. Thomas Aquinas as "disembodied intelligences." We are embodied, with a physical body and with social belonging. What God wants for us is that we shall become truly and fully human. A contemporary Christian theologian, Paul Lehmann, has phrased it well: "God's purpose for us is to make us and keep us human." And if God is to make that possible for us, God must somehow share in our human experience in the terms which are natural and proper to us all.

The thinkers of the early Church expressed this requirement

in a phrase well-known in theological circles: "What God has not assumed, that he has not redeemed." *Assumed:* taken to himself and made part of his own life; *redeemed:* given wholeness to human existence. The insight of Christian faith is that in Jesus, God so acted that God can be seen as sharing in, even as living, a genuine human life in its every aspect, save for sin which is not essential to us but is a defect in us. So Jesus could be, and was, thirsty, both as a matter of being like us embodied physically and also as a participant mentally, emotionally, and psychologically, in our social existence as men and women.

I just said 'save for sin' and by that I pointed at the one thing that was true of him as it is not true for you and me. Whereas we are continually in defection from God's intention for us, seeking our own way, disobedient to the 'heavenly vision' — in fact sinners — Jesus as a man was always open to God, always doing what God purposed for him, and always obedient as a faithful Son to the vocation which God had given him. Because he was in this way truly and fully human, he has been called 'the *Proper* Man,' using that adjective 'proper' in its correct sense of 'genuine', made entirely actual and concrete. Jesus was human as God intends human existence to be.

Now we cannot demonstrate this from the gospel narratives. They do not provide us with complete details of Jesus' life. To say that Jesus is the 'Proper Man' is to speak from faith. It is faith which responds to the witness which we find in the gospels, written as they were 'from faith' (that of those who knew most directly about Jesus) and 'to faith' (that of those who on their part make that early witness their own). It is impossible to speak 'christianly' without such faith. The assertions about Jesus, like those about the God who sent him, are not demonstrable like statements about the angles of a triangle or like the conclusions of a logical argument. Yet faith is not irrational or absurd. It is "reason grown courageous," as somebody once put it, going beyond demonstrable truths to those that are vital and vivid and evocative of our best response to what our life, our history, and our world present to us.

Because Jesus is the 'Proper Man,' he is for us the pattern for all humanity. Since he is that pattern, yet by having no special manhood entirely different from our own, Jesus *shames* us. He makes us conscious of our failures and of how far we fall short of what we should be, by and under God's gracious help. He does more than that, however. Not only is he the *pattern* of true human life, as a loving and caring and dutiful son of his and our heavenly Father. He is also the one from whom flows the *power* for us to be changed and to become like him. So we might say that as pattern he is a disclosure of what we are meant by God to become, while as power he enables us to move on to become just that. The ancient Fathers of the Church had a fine way of saying this: that in and by Jesus you and I and all other men and women can become *filii in Filio* — 'sons in *the* Son.'

Historically the Church has used two theological terms to state this: Incarnation and Atonement. We may not wish to use them today; we may think that we have found other and for us more suitable expressions. But the point they make is clear. 'Incarnation' says that in Jesus, more than anywhere else so far as we know, God is sharing our human existence in exactly the way that we know it and experience it; 'Atonement' says that in consequence of that sharing God is making it possible for us to be one with the divine purpose, delivered from all that would prevent us from achieving our destiny as true sons and daughters of God. "In Christ," St. Paul tells us, "God was reconciling the world unto himself."

9.

It Is Finished

It is unfortunate that the first translators of the Bible into English used here the word 'finished' in their effort to put into our own language what the original Greek word of the New Testament is saying. For the Greek word signifies 'finished' in a sense not common with us today but entirely different in meaning. For us 'finished' is a way of saying that something is over, has ended, has come to a stop. But the Greek word says what to-day we might better put as ''accomplished.' That is, it tells us something like this: 'The work has been done and in doing it there has been accomplished what God had in view and what God purposed.' It is as if Jesus were saying, 'I have done my job; I have fulfilled my vocation; I have completed what was given me to do; I have brought to a trimphant conclusion the purpose or intention for which I was born, for which I have lived, and for which God sent me into the world.'

To say *that* is very different indeed from saying, 'Well, that has come to an end, that life of mine; there is nothing else to follow it.' For the things that Jesus said and did have not come to a stop; there was a great deal to follow. What was to follow was the continued bringing of Jesus' fellow-humans into a relationship with God through what Jesus did, in a communion or fellowship with God and their fellow-humans which is so much

41

a reality, so strong and invincible, that nothing can break it down. That community or fellowship is what we mean or ought to mean when we talk about 'the Church.' The Church is a society of men and women who so fully belong to God and are so richly given God's gracious presence that it differs from any other human grouping. As the New Testament tells us, it is the Body of Christ, a social humanity which carries on what Christ did in ''the days of his flesh'' when he was visibly with us for some thirty years. He is *still* with us; but now he has been ''let loose into the world'' where nothing and nobody can stop him; and he has taken us up into himself so that we may continue to do his work in the world.

Earlier in these meditations I quoted some words of a Christian saint of the Middle Ages: ''The entire life of Christ was the mystery of the cross.'' I ask you now to consider how appropriate those words are in connection with this saying from the cross: ''It is finished'' — ''My work has been accomplished, my vocation has been worked out; I have done to the very limit what I came to do.''

In St. John's gospel there is the story of the evening before Jesus was betrayed and given up into the hands of men. You will recall how the story tells us that on that occasion Jesus washed the feet of his disciples. The story in St. John is prefaced by this comment, ''Having loved his own which were in the world, he loved them unto the end.'' In the original Greek of St. John's gospel 'unto the end' does not mean that he loved them until his death. The Greek phrase is *eis telos.* What the passage means is this: ''Having loved his own in the world, he loved them *to the very limit.* '' That is, Jesus loved them to the utmost degree that it was at all possible for anybody to love. His love for them, and through them for us too, was not partial nor occasional; it was a love that knew no boundaries, no limits, and had no stop; it was an enduring and everlasting love.

So at every moment in his days in Palestine, the whole of it being a foreshadowing of the complete offering of himself

42

on the cross, Jesus loved, loved to the very limit, with a love that never failed. Everybody whom he met he loved; and in every circumstance in which he found himself he did the loving thing. That is the witness which is given in the gospel narratives. In loving in that supreme fashion, he offered himself to others as he offered himself to God. That is what sacrifice is all about. St. Augustine, the great Christian thinker of the fourth and fifth centuries, defined sacrifice as an offering to God whose purpose is to open up, enable, and establish a new relationship between God and human kind. Thus the whole life of Jesus was an offering of himself to God, as it was also a giving of himself as an offering to everybody he met. In that way, God and human existence are brought together in a decisive way. Jesus gave himself to God his Father; and on God's behalf and acting for God he gave himself to men and women and children, to make available for them all a communion and fellowship together with God and under God, whose distinctive quality was a sharing in love. But, to repeat what I have urged earlier, for this to happen there must be not only a love shared with the divine Lover who is God, but also a love shared with other people. For only when we live in love with God *and* with others are we really living. An English poet has put this well: "Not where I breathe but where I love, I live." True life is love worked out in act.

Of course we must be clear about what meaning we give to the word 'love.' All too often it suggests to us sentimentality or a merely emotional liking. But the real meaning of love is not such sentimentality nor emotion. Rather, love is giving gladly and receiving gladly; it is mutuality or sharing; it is a gracious openness to other people and a readiness to enter into their lives, living with them in their sadness as well as in their joy, in their agony as well as in their ecstacy. God's love is that; our love is intended to become that.

The whole course of Jesus' life was just such love, expressed in his words and deeds, in all that he did and in all that he said.

His vocation was to manifest such love; this was what he had been sent to do. On the cross, this human loving was brought to its climactic point and was placarded before the world, so that all people might respond to it and become new and renewed men and women in Christ. On the cross, then, Jesus did in a vivid fashion what he was always doing. In his total self-giving, his complete sacrifice of self, he released into the world the divine, the cosmic, the ultimate Love which is nothing other than God.

We who dare to call ourselves Christ's people can now respond to and share in the love that Jesus released into our sinful, distorted, perverse, and unjust world. We can be caught up into what older theologies sometimes and not too happily called "the finished work of Christ." For us to be caught up into and share in Christ's work is to make our own willing answer to what Jesus did there and then. We who are potential lovers are to become genuine lovers, open to others, reflecting God's own love, and ready to be instruments for God's love here and now, in this contemporary world — in the place and at a time when hatred, malice, pride, injustice, oppression, and all manner of evil are present. Our Christian task, then, can be put very simply. *God's* grace given to us is to become *our* daily endeavour to act out, in concrete ways, the love which alone can make this world a fit place for the sons and daughters of the divine Lover.

10.

Into Thy Hands

The work of Jesus, his fulfilling of his heavenly Father's vocation for him, had been accomplished. He had given himself utterly to God in obedience to that vocation; and his giving of himself had led to his death on the cross. Yet that death, death to self and to all merely worldly aspirations, was no incidental affair; rather, it was (as we have seen) the culmination of the self-giving which had characterized all that had gone before, certainly from the day when after his baptism by John in Jordan he had realized just what his vocation was to be, just what sort of work he had been called to do.

Now, as the moment of actual dying drew near, there is only one thing more than he can do. He can commend or commit his vocation, his work, and himself to the God who was with him and to whom he had dedicated himself. He can do this as a man, without reserve of any kind, in a complete offering for God to use as God alone could do. So he said, as early Christian tradition reports the last word spoken from the cross, "Into *thy* hands I commend [or commit] my spirit." (Luke 23:46)

Let us be quite clear that on the cross Jesus was in one sense at least — the physical sense — unable to do anything which would be visible to human eyes. He was nailed to the cross; he hung there unmovable upon it; he could not 'come down'

45

from it. Yet there was one thing Jesus could do; *and he did it*. He could commit all that he had done during his days in Palestine and all that had been done to him to the God who was his loving Father. In doing this, we dare to say, he 'saved the world.' That is how Christian faith has always understood Jesus' death upon the cross. Let me repeat it. Jesus was helpless, unable to act further in any obvious way, entirely at the disposal of those who had condemned him and had now crucified him. He could do nothing, *except save the world*.

What can possibly be meant by that statement? What can it mean to affirm that Jesus on the cross saves the world? Can any such affirmation make sense to us today? Or is it only a traditional and for us today senseless bit of language that our ancestors used and that for them had a genuine significance although for us it sounds absurd? We cannot evade such questions. Least of all can we evade them if we would be honest with ourselves and with God whose every word is truth. That is why I now urge upon us all an interpretation which does not make sense, to me surely and I hope to those who hear it.

If we enquire about our basic human problem, beneath and behind the obvious problems we face in our personal relationships, in our lives as members of human society, in our national and international worries, in our economic and political and practical human existence, what answer can we give? Surely our basic human problem is exactly what the great German reformer Martin Luther once said it was: "We are twisted in upon our selves." In Latin, which was the language he used here, *incurvati in se*. Everyone of us, young or old, clever or simple, black or white or yellow in skin, in the twentieth century and in any other century, in the United States or Russia or China or Britain — everyone of us is 'curved in' or 'twisted in' upon himself or herself. That is to say, we are *self*-centred. Not just in the necessary fashion which is essential to each of us if we are to be truly ourselves, psychologically and physiologically; we are self-centred in a false and destructive way. For you and I are people who 'want what we want when we want it,' as a popular song of the earlier part of this century put it. Even when we are at our best, unconcern for others and focussing upon ourselves still persist. If you and I look honestly at ourselves, we are obliged to admit that what I have just said is indeed the truth about you as it is about me.

Since that is our basic human problem, we need to be released from such false concentration upon self. There is only one way in which such release can come. That way was defined years ago by a Scots writer who said that if we are ever to be released we must have some possibility of knowing "the expulsive power of a new affection." Or, in quite simple words, we have got to be loved, loved utterly and completely, loved just as we are and loved for what we might become. Only in that fashion can we be opened up, given a power to respond, enabled to become new people who do not centre everything upon their own little selves.

On the cross Jesus revealed precisely that utter and complete love, crowning by his dying an entire life of self-giving love. In him we witness the very disclosure of acceptance and through that acceptance the expression of the expulsive power of love. But for Christian faith, Jesus did more than reveal or disclose this. He enacted it. Jesus was the human enactment, in the existence which is common to all men and women everywhere, of a Love that never fails, a Love to which we can make genuine response, a Love that we can entirely trust, a Love that continues in spite of all that might obstruct or deny it. A familiar hymn speaks of that Love: "Just as I am, they Love unknown, has broken every barrier down." *Every barrier:* everything which would make impossible our becoming truly God's children who live in God's love and therefore are made whole. In the familiar phrase, 'we are saved.' We are saved *from* the falsity of living to ourselves alone and saved *to* the truth of living in loving relationships. We are saved *from* lovelessness *to* the capacity of loving. Another hymn says it well: "Love to

47

the loveless shown, that they may lovely be.'' 'Lovely' is a word that means both able to love and also attractive to others in our loving.

As Jesus commended or committed himself and his whole work, his vocation, to God who is the great cosmic Lover, so he also committed or commended to God all of us, you and me, who have been drawn to him as he hangs on his cross. So we make bold to say, when we have done or sought to do the truly loving and hence truly human thing, and have been desperately conscious of failure, frustration, and rejection, as he was on the cross — when we have done all that we can, we can be bold to say too, ''Father, into thy hands I commit myself'' — and I can commit myself, because through Jesus Christ my Lord, my Master, my Saviour, I have been grasped and held by God's love, that will keep me, now and forever.

Epilogue:

Our three hours with Jesus on his cross are now over. Jesus has died, not simply as the victim of human wrongdoing, although he *was* its victim, but as the *Victor* over that wrongdoing. ''The powers of hell have done their worst.'' Certainly they have done that. But Jesus has not been defeated, because he has accepted and endured. And so, in the words of a great hymn from the early days of the Church, ''God is reigning from the Tree.'' What another ancient hymn calls ''the glorious battle'' over human wrong has come to its bitter end; and the end, although it has been most appallingly bitter, has been a triumphant end.

Christian faith proclaims this. 'God is reigning,' not from some sapphire throne remote from you and me and remote from our human condition of suffering and despair and death. No, God is reigning, as sovereign Lord, from *the Tree* — that is to say, God reigns as sovereign Lord at the very point in which

48

human wickedness, human wrong, and human despair, seem to be most triumphant. Here is the strange and paradoxical assertion of Christian faith. How is this to be understood?

In St. Paul's Cathedral in London, before the damage done during the Second World War, there was a great crucifix behind the High Altar, showing the body of Jesus hanging on the cross. Above that crucifix in letters of gold were these Latin words: *Sic deus dilexit mundum* — 'So God loved the world.' God loved the world *in that way,* it says. God loved it so deeply, so truly, with such unbelievable passion, that God gave us all the One in whom God acted decisively, vividly, supremely, so "that whosoever believeth in *him* should not perish but have everlasting life."

For you and me Good Friday is the time and opportunity to give ourselves afresh, as "a reasonable, holy, and living sacrifice," so that thus dedicating ourselves, we are open to allow into our little and defective human lives the divine Love "that will not let us go." The Love that hangs on the cross, that human loving which was the human life of Jesus, is the reflexion and agency for the divine loving that is the very God whose "nature and whose name is Love." The last line of Dante's *Divine Comedy* runs this way in the original Italian: *L'amore che muove il sole e le altre stelle,* Italian words that have often been called the most beautiful words in the most beautiful language spoken by humans. Even in English, 'the Love that moves the sun and the other stars,' they are striking both in their beauty and in their meaning. God is that Love; that Love is God.

For those of us who have sought to respond and who still continue to seek to respond to the events of Good Friday, something more must be said. The Love that 'moves the sun and the other stars' is also the Love that moves *us.* It enters into us and it works unceasingly upon us. In the death of Jesus on the cross, in his victory over sin and evil and death, that Love has got into our lives and has re-made those lives. God

49

began this process of loving towards humankind when the first human creatures came to be; God has continued to do it in many different ways through the ages, often enough in ways that have not been recognized for what they really are. God did it supremely on Good Friday, with a speciality and with a vividness and an intensity that are unknown elsewhere. God does it today, again with decisiveness and vividness and intensity, as we are drawn to the One who hung on the cross. Such Love, such a Lover, can never be defeated. The Love of God in Christ Jesus our Lord was not overcome and destroyed on that Friday centuries ago. Rather, it was 'let loose into the world' where it can never be stopped.

On Easter Day we shall see its victory because on Easter morning it was shown for what it always is: "the power of God unto salvation for everyone who believes." So, as we end our three hours of meditation and prayer, let us acclaim the triumphant Lord:

> *All hail the power of Jesus' name!*
> *Let angels prostrate fall;*
> *To him all majesty ascribe,*
> *And crown him Lord of all.*

11.

Holy Saturday

This is a day of expectation and anticipation.

It is a day of *expectation* in the proper meaning of that word. It is not, that is to say, a day when we look forward wistfully and pathetically to something which we trust may come to pass. Rather, it is a day in which we eagerly, gratefully, and earnestly look toward the plain manifestation of God's victory in Christ when, on the first Easter morning, Jesus "risen from the dead" was revealed to "chosen witnesses" as the Lord who had been "let loose into the world," triumphant over sin and evil and death.

Again, it is a day of *anticipation,* also in the proper sense of that word. It is not that we are looking towards something which will be entirely novel and unexpected. It is anticipation in that it gives expression, although by intimation and sugges- tion, to something that will be fully manifest on Easter Day. Now, on this day between Good Friday and Easter, if we may talk chronologically about it, we are already glimpsing the manifest triumph of Jesus Christ whom God has raised from the dead.

On such a day, when (as one of the old collects says) we learn that it is "through the grave and gate of death" that we are brought to share in what that same collect styles "our joyful resurrection,'' it is appropriate that we should think for a while about the fact of death, and with it judgement and the significance of hell and heaven. Those four — death, judgement, hell, and heaven — are often called 'the last things.' Usually they are associated with the traditional season of Advent, before Christmas, yet I believe that they are equally properly seen in connection with the Good-Friday-Easter paradigm of Christian faith, in which our thoughts naturally and rightly turn to our own human destiny.

Thus we can begin by saying something about death. An old proverb has it that the only certain things are death and taxes. Which is to say, we all die. To die is human; everyone dies. But not only does everyone die; *all* of us dies. In authentic Christian understanding it is not a matter of a body dying while something called 'the soul' does not die. To think and talk in that fashion is to be unbiblical. For the Bible knows nothing of any such divided humanity. Body-and-soul talk is Hellenistic, not biblical. Unhappily, many Christian people and some Christian theologians have been Hellenistic in their interpretation rather than truly biblical. For the Bible we die as total humans, who as human are a strange complex of body and mind and hence we are as much our bodies as we are our minds (or spirits or souls, if you wish to use those terms).

To know that we must die and that all we are must die is to be realistic. What happens to us, then, is exactly what happened to our Lord Jesus Christ, who died like the rest of us, thus demonstrating his full sharing in our human lot. But not only do we die; we are judged or appraised. Every moment of our lives we are being judged, to be sure. We judge ourselves and others judge us as we judge others. More than that, however; we are appraised by God who knows us better than we can know ourselves and can judge accurately what we have done and what we are. We are judged by God daily; we are also judged or appraised by God '' at the hour of our death.'' What has each one of us really amounted to, through the whole

52

course of our earthly existence, as God understands it? How much or how little have we contributed to the purpose of God and its fulfillment? How do we stand up to that appraisal? Here too our Lord Jesus Christ was judged. While *we* are shown up by such appraisal to be poor, weak, fallible, and defective in the way in which we have played our part in the achievement of God's purpose, *he* is shown to have been faithful and obedient to the vocation which was his.

Then there is hell. Hell was once defined by William Morris, the English artist and essayist and craftsman, as "absence of fellowship." We have all been in hell, in that sense, time and time again, since we have refused fellowship and have chosen to live to ourselves and for ourselves. Jesus did not experience *that* hell, for his whole life was one of fellowship with others as with God. But he did know hell in another sense. Hell is a feeling of frustration and defeat; and that feeling he experienced as he hung on the cross. As we have seen, the cry "My God, my God, why hast thou forsaken me?" can be taken to tell us just that. Such a 'hell' is worse than anything else that can happen to us. But for Jesus, and because of Jesus for us too, it need only be a passing sensation, provided we see through it to God's victory over, yet never in spite of, such tragic moments as all of us have known or can know.

And 'heaven' is true fulfillment. To my mind our best way of grasping the meaning of heaven is to consider how God accepts and receives us, just as we are and for what we have done, into the divine life. God who is Love makes us part of that divine life, so that words from one of St. Peter's epistles come alive: we are made "partakers of the divine nature." That is a possible destiny for us, just as hell, or absence of fellowship with God and our human brothers and sisters, is also a possible destiny whose horror we can feel so deeply and painfully. To be received into God's life: is not that what we believe took place for Jesus? And is not that the sense which we ought to give to all talk about the 'resurrection' of our whole personality, body and soul. In Jesus that is what we see taking place. This is what will be manifested on Easter morning and this is what already we anticipate today, before that Easter manifestation.

To live as a Christian is to live in hope, in real expectation. But our hope is not in and for the good things which one day we may be given in some heavenly state. Christian hopes is *in God,* not in what we should like to get from God. St. Francis de Sales said that "we are to hope in the God of consolations, not in the consolations of God." His saying should never be forgotten. To hope in God is to live in the eager expectation that we shall be incorporated into God's ongoing loving activity, in creation and redemption, come what may. This is why, as Kirsopp Lake once put it, "Faith is not belief in spite of evidence but life in scorn of consequence." And what faith is, so also is hope.

Tomorrow, Easter Day, we shall be thinking of "our joyful resurrection." *Our* resurrection is to share in *Christ's* resurrection. It is to be taken, with him and in him, the very life of God the great Lover of us all. Thus our resurrection will be to dwell with Christ forever and always with God and in God, however this may be accomplished — and about the details of that reception we are ignorant and ought not to presume to make a diagram. It is also part of our resurrection to be with Christ as he is 'let loose into the world,' participating in the ceaseless creative and redemptive work of God.

On Easter we shall be celebrating that we can and do live in Christ as he lives in us, so that we have the inestimable privilege of serving as his fellow-workers in the 'amorization' of all things. To serve in that way demands from us that we shall be those through whom God's gracious and unyielding love is available to more people, at more places, at more times, and in more ways. Which means that we are joined with God in Christ as God strives for justice for all men and women and children, fights oppression and unrighteousness wherever they are found, and pours wonderful and divine love into the lives of all of us human children — if only we will accept it and respond to it.

12.

Easter Day

In the Epistle to the Colossians there are these words: "If ye then be risen with Christ, seek those things which are above, where Christ sitteth on the right hand of God."

On Easter Day, Christians in every part of the world commemorate the victory of their Lord Jesus Christ over death and evil and sin. Not that Easter is a denial or negation of the horrible fact of Good Friday, when a combination of political power, ecclesiastical intolerance, and public indifference brought to his death the One whom succeeding generations have regarded as the best man who ever lived. Easter does not overturn the awful reality of that Friday. What it does, as St. John's gospel makes plain, is declare that in the suffering, anguish, and apparent defeat of that man, God disclosed himself in act for what he always is, what he is always up to, what God is always doing in the world.

So for the whole life of Christ we can use some words by Alfred North Whitehead, in his book *Adventures of Ideas:* "The essence of Christianity is the appeal to the life of Christ as a revelation of the nature of God and of his agency in the world...There can be no doubt as to what elements in the record have evoked a response from all that is best in human nature:

the Mother, the Child, and the bare manger; the lowly man, homeless and self-forgetful, with his message of peace, love, and sympathy; the suffering, the agony, the tender words as life ebbed, the final despair: *and the whole with the authority of supreme victory."*

I have stressed those last words, for Whitehead rightly saw and said that the conclusion of the matter was not a defeat which would lead us to feel pity for the one who died on the cross, but was supreme victory. As an old teacher of mine once put it, "Despite, or rather because of, all the anguish and suffering, Jesus strides through the stories about him as a victor, not as a victim; as conquering, not as vanquished." It is that triumph, that conquering Love, which we celebrate on Easter Day.

Any preacher who dares to talk as if that great day, and the resurrection of Christ which it commemorates and celebrates, is all about 'the flowers that bloom in the spring' and the renewal of life and nature in springtime after the darkness of winter, is talking sheer nonsense. Indeed we might quote words from Gilbert and Sullivan back at him, "The flowers that bloom in the spring have nothing to do with the case." Or if they have anything to do with it, it is only as a symbol of newness of life after apparent death.

Easter is the day when we gratefully and adoringly praise God that in and through defeat and death, through suffering and anguish, there is the demonstration of divine Love enacted on the stage of human existence. That Love, the divine and everlasting Love that God himself *is,* cannot be put down or destroyed. 'Through the grave and gate of death', as we remembered on Holy Saturday, that Love comes to its 'joyous resurrection' and shows that it 'cannot be holden of death.' To be sure the reality of death is still there. In the heavenly places, we might put it in a 'story-way' of speaking, the risen Lord still is also the Lord who was crucified. Wesley's hymn has it right:

> *Those dear tokens of his passion*
> *Still his glorious body bears;*
> *Cause of endless exultation*
> *To his ransomed worshippers.*

Easter Day not only affirms the triumph of the enacted love of God in Christ Jesus. It also affirms that in this victory you and I are given more than the disclosure that divine love triumphs through human defeat; we are given the assurance that each one of us and all of us together, who respond with heart and will and mind, share in that triumph. We too are "risen with Christ," whose total human existence is now and forever taken into the life of God, where "Christ sitteth at the right hand of God." Thus Easter is not only *God's* victory in Christ. It is *our* victory too, because we who have been caught up into Christ are now risen with him. Our humanity, poor and feeble and defective as we know it to be, is in and with God. No matter what happens to us through "the changes and chances of this mortal life," our hearts can be and should be, and are, taken into God. Having thus been taken into God, they are for God to use so that the divine purpose of loving concern, with greater justice and sharing in love, may be more fully and adequately worked out in this world of ours — this world of ours which is also God's world.

The text from Colossians, with which we began, goes on to say something that on Easter Day we must emphasize. Since we men and women are risen with Christ, we are "to seek those things which are above." That does not imply that we are to reject the world or to be indifferent to it and to what goes on within it for good or for ill. What it does declare to us is that our perspective, our outlook, our stance, is to be so much identified with God defined in Christ that we live here and now "as seeing him who is invisible" and that we understand ourselves and God in the light of what has been done in Christ. It asserts that in Christ's death and resurrection a window has been opened so that we now can see God and the things of God in a new way.

We see God... but *how* do we see God? We see God now, if we are truly "in the faith of Christ," as the great Lover of the creation who is with us in sadness and in gladness and will never let us go. We shall have problems, troubles, worries, difficulties, obstacles, perils, threats, and tragedy in our lives. That is sure to be the case. We are not miraculously delivered from any of these. Yet we need never be afraid, for "in every respect God works towards a good end for those who love him." So St. Paul says and Christian faith dares to agree with the Apostle. You and I are *safe,* not in an obvious and worldly sense but in an abiding and eternal sense.

We see God; we also see ourselves. *How* do we see ourselves, in the light of the Easter triumph? We see ourselves, now that we are risen with Christ and forever with him in the Father, as God's dear children, each one of us different in many ways from any other and each one of us with his or her own character and possibility. We see ourselves as on the way to becoming truly human — and that is the same as saying created, finite, mortal lovers-in-the-making. We see ourselves as God's agents in the world, seeking to make that world a place of love and justice where each man and woman can find what Jewish tradition calls *shalom,* rich and abundant life in community with our fellow humans.

Human life, taken with Christ into God, becomes what by creation it was meant to be: we are "heirs of God and joint-heirs with Christ, if so be that we suffer with him, to the end that we may also be glorified together." Another ancient prayer tells us something more demanding: that as we receive "Christ's inestimable benefits," so also through his grace we are "to endeavour ourselves to follow the blessed steps of his most holy life." That is the challenge of Easter Day for you and me.

13.

After Easter

After Easter — and I am not talking just of the days in what in church circles we call 'Eastertide,' the period between Easter Day and the Ascension Day with Whitsunday or the Feast of Pentecost at its end. There is that church-season of Eastertide, to be sure; and it ought to be observed joyously by Christian people. But what I am now talking about is the whole of our human existence in what might be styled the post-Easter life. The excitement and thrill of Easter have gone; we are now in a less exultant mood and can think in a more tranquil fashion about what has happened.

Years ago I heard an amusing little story which makes the point. A newspaper reporter was in the habit of enquiring of local clergy what was happening in their several churches, so that the Saturday issue of his newspaper might have an appropriate item. It happened that during Easter week the reporter asked a vicar what was to take place next Sunday. To which the reply came, "Well, next Sunday is Low Sunday, in the octave of Easter, and we're going to repeat the Easter music." When the item appeared in the newspaper, it said: "Next Sunday, in such-and-such a church, the Easter music will be repeated one octave lower." That ridiculous story suggests something that we need to consider.

One octave lower, yes. With less excitement, less thrill, less exultation, the time after Easter is a time to consider seriously where we are; what we are about as 'the Easter people,' to use a fine phrase employed some years back by English Roman Catholic bishops in a public pronouncement; and what is the significance for us here-and-now of the Easter triumph.

Already we have seen one thing. Easter means that we have been privileged to learn that the divine Love acted in deed and event, not in word only, to show that such divine Love is available to everybody and that nothing can stop its work in the world, however ghastly that world may seem to be. Such divine Love "could not be holden of death" nor could it be stopped or put aside.

Now if there is any one thing that you and I want to know, as we observe and experience what is wrong, sinful, and evil in the world and in ourselves, it is that the *last word* is not with such things but rather is found in a Love that is undefeated and ceaselessly at work. We need the assurance that in the end the true victory belongs not to hatred and injustice, lovelessness and carelessness, all of which we know so well, but with God — and that is a way of saying that life in caring and with concern, seeking the right and just things, is also undefeated and ultimately will be victorious. Without that assurance we feel that our human existence is pointless and absurd, without enduring value or significance.

Here theories and speculations are of little help. All they can do is indicate what the best men and women of our race have always hoped for, desired, and wanted. The Easter message tells us that these hopes, desires, and wants are not vain and stupid. It points to a fact, ploughed into history: that Jesus was not destroyed by the wickedness of men and women but that through the experience of Good Friday the Love of God, in the human loving of Jesus, emerged triumphant. For you and me, that means that we can live in the confidence that our human existence has value and worth and that our inevitable struggles, our undeniable problems, and our inescapable fears, do not have the last word. So as I have said again and again, we need never be afraid, in any ultimate sense. It is not obvious that things will be right; and only an unrealistic fool would think that life becomes simple and easy. Yet in this 'after Easter' time — for all the rest of our days — we may have the sure confidence that "the stars in their courses" (as the Old Testament puts it in describing a battle of long ago) fight with us for the "everlasting right" which is God's purpose for his children.

•

Easter Day has come and gone, but Easter victory remains. Never should we permit anybody to tell us that Easter is all about the personal immortality of the soul; and that this is its main message. No, not at all. Rather, it is the assurance that we can live here, now, without death claiming dominion over us. It is the assurance, given to our faith, that evil will have no final victory, wrong no enduring conquest. In that faith you and I can live confidently, courageously, daring to trust in the love of God. We can live with a light heart and an almost reckless readiness to care and serve and give. We are secure in God, forever. We are freed from "faithless fears and worldly anxieties." And in the end, God will take us into the divine life, precisely because we have committed ourselves to God defined in (because enacted for us by) Jesus Christ. That is the destiny promised to those who know the joy of Christ's resurrection. Alleluia!

About the author

W. Norman Pittenger, distinguished preacher, prolific author and professor of theology, spent more than thirty years on the faculty of the General Seminary in New York. Since 1966 he has taught at Cambridge University, England, while keeping up a heavy schedule of preaching engagements and lecture trips in other parts of the world. *Passion and Perfection* is reported to be his eighty-second book.